CW00383578

THE
POCKET

Cockney
Rhyming Slang

Published in 2024
by Gemini Adult Books Ltd
Part of Gemini Books Group

Based in Woodbridge and London

Marine House, Tide Mill Way
Woodbridge, Suffolk IP12 1AP
United Kingdom

www.geminibooks.com

Text and Design © 2024 Gemini Books Group
Part of the Gemini Pocket series

ISBN 978-1-91708-295-2

A CIP catalogue record for this book is available from the British Library.

Disclaimer: The book is a guidebook purely for information and entertainment
purposes only. All trademarks, individual and company names, brand names,
registered names, quotations, celebrity names, logos, dialogues and catchphrases
used or cited in this book are the property of their respective owners. The
publisher does not assume and hereby disclaims any liability to any party for any
loss, damage or disruption caused by errors or omissions, whether such errors
or omissions result from negligence, accident or any other cause. This book is an
unofficial and unauthorised publication by Gemini Adult Books Ltd and has not
been licensed, approved, sponsored or endorsed by any person or entity.

Printed in China

10 9 8 7 6 5 4 3 2 1

Cover: Wikimedia Commons. Images: Adobe: 83. Freepik.com: 4, 13, 14, 19, 28, 34,
47, 67, 87. Shutterstock.com: Blueee77, 20; neftali, 33; Odin Illustration, 39; Qualit
Design, 43; Alexander_P, 51; MaKars, 71; Danussa, 59; Roman Bykhalov, 75;
Victoria Sergeeva, 83; SofiaV, 95. Wikimedia Commons: 3, 7, 34, 55, 63, 79, 91, 99.

THE POCKET

Cockney Rhyming Slang

G:

Contents

Introduction

Conventionally, a cockney is anyone born 'within the sound of Bow Bells' – St Mary-le-Bow church, in London – but rather than fixating on Dirty Den from *EastEnders*, Dickensian villains or Pearly Kings and Queens, perhaps we should focus rather on comedian Arthur Smith's definition, which may be nearer the mark: a cockney is simply a 'non-posh Londoner'.

This pocket glossary is intended for quick and easy reference; it's a portable cockney kit. Supposedly, cockney rhyming slang was originally invented to outwit authority and eavesdroppers. Whether that's true or not, it remains a closed language to the uninitiated. But its humour is too good to be missed, which is, in large part, the rationale for this compact, entertaining volume.

Very rarely does a true cockney use his or her 'loaf of bread' (head); a cockney uses simply their 'loaf'. Where slang is abbreviated in this way, examples are given. Of course, cockney rhyming slang is constantly evolving and being added to, so this pocket guide cannot be the last word, but it offers a dependably solid foundation.

St Mary-le-Bow church

COCKNEY

–

ENGLISH

COCKNEY	ENGLISH
Abergavenny	penny
Adam and Eve	believe
Adam and the Ants	pants
Adrian Mole	dole – 'He's on the Adrian.'
advice from Mother	rubber (condom)
airs and graces	faces, braces, Epsom Races
air gunner	stunner
à la mode	code
alderman's nail	tail – ''e's wagging 'is alderman's.'
alligator	later
almond rocks	socks – 'Me almonds need darning.'
Al Pacino	cappuccino
Andy Cain	rain

Acker Bilk

milk

Acker Bill was an English clarinettist, who had a distinctive goatee beard and wore a bowler hat and striped waistcoat. His instrumental 'Stranger on the Shore' was the UK's bestselling single in 1962.

apples and pears

stairs

Said to be from fruit displayed by
greengrocers or barrow-boys in front
of their stores or stalls in 'steps and stairs'.
Also used to refer to an appearance in court,
from the stairs leading from the cell to
the dock in an Old Bailey court.

COCKNEY	ENGLISH
Anna Maria	fire (domestic)
'apenny dip	ship – 'The *QE2*'s a fair-sized 'apenny!'
apple fritter	bitter (beer)
April Fool's	stools, tools, pools (gambling)
April showers	flowers
Aristotle	bottle
Army and Navy	gravy
Artful Dodger	lodger
Auntie Ella	umbrella
Auntie Nellie	belly

COCKNEY	ENGLISH
babbling brook	cook, or crook
Bacardi Breezer	geezer
bacon and eggs	legs – 'Wot smashin' bacons!'
bag for life	wife
ball of chalk	walk
ball of fat	cat
balloon car	saloon bar – 'Meet me in the balloon.'
band in the box	pox
Barack Obama	pyjamas
Barnaby Rudge	judge
Barnet Fair	hair – 'Must get me barnet cut.'
bat and wicket	ticket
Bath bun	son, or sun

band of hope

soap

The Band of Hope was a society which promoted lifelong abstention from alcohol among young people, founded in Britain in 1847.

Bananarama

drama

COCKNEY	ENGLISH
basin of gravy	baby
battle-cruiser	boozer (pub)
bazaar	bar (pub)
bear's paw	saw (tool)
Beecham's pill	bill – 'Show me the Beecham's' – or a still (photograph)
bees and honey	money – 'I ain't got the bees to pay me rent.'
beggar my neighbour	on the Labour (Labour Exchange, dole)
bird lime	time (as in 'doing time', in prison)
biscuits and cheese	knees – 'She ain't 'arf got knobbly biscuits.'
bladder of lard	card
Boat Race	face

COCKNEY	ENGLISH
Bob Marley	charlie (cocaine)
bob squash	a wash
Bo-Peep	sleep
boracic lint	skint (broke) – 'I'm boracic!'
borrow and beg	egg
bottle and glass	arse – ''e pinched me bottle!'
bottle and stopper	copper, police officer
bow and arrow(s)	sparrow(s)
box of toys	noise
Brad Pitt	fit
bread and butter	gutter
bread and cheese	sneeze
Bristol City	'titty,' breast – 'A fine pair of Bristols.'
Britney Spears	tears

COCKNEY	ENGLISH
Brussels' sprouts	scouts – 'Young 'Arry's joined the Brussels'.'
bubble and squeak	beak (magistrate)
bucket and pail	jail
bull and cow	row (argue)
burnt cinder	'winder' (window)
Burton-on-Trent	rent – 'I 'ave to pay me Burton every week.'
bushel and peck	neck
Bushy Park	lark (joke)
butcher's hook	look – 'Let's 'ave a butcher's at it.'

COCKNEY	ENGLISH
Cain and Abel	table
canal boat	tote
Cape of Good Hope	soap
Captain Cook	book
Catherine Zeta-Jones	moans
carving knife	wife
cash and carried	married
cat and mouse	house
Chalk Farm	arm
cheerful giver	liver
Chevy Chase	face – ''e's got a gloomy sort of Chevy.'
china plate	mate – ''e's me best china.'
chop sticks	six (bingo call)
clever mike	bike

can't keep still

treadmill

The treadmill was a nineteenth-century punishment in which prisoners would be forced to walk without stopping on a treadmill, which could accommodate several prisoners at the same time.

COCKNEY	ENGLISH
clickety-click	sixty-six (bingo call)
coals and coke	broke
cobbler's awls	balls (testicles) – 'It's cold enough to freeze yer cobbler's.'
cock linnet	minute (time)
cock sparrow	barrow
cocoa	say-so

cherry hog

dog – 'Me cherry's 'aving pups.'

It was common in the nineteenth century
for Londoners to travel to Kent during
the summer to help with picking hops,
where 'cherry' became a slang term for
a dog, from the 'cherry hog' container
used to collect the hops.

COCKNEY	ENGLISH
cockney breakfast	gin or brandy and soda water
Cockneyland	London
cockroach	coach
Conan Doyle	boil (verb and noun)
cop a flower pot	'cop it hot', get into trouble
country cousin	dozen
crowded space	suitcase
crust of bread	head – 'Use yer crust!'
cuddle and kiss	miss (a girl)
currant bun	son, or sun
custard and jelly	telly (television)
cut and carried	married
cuts and scratches	matches

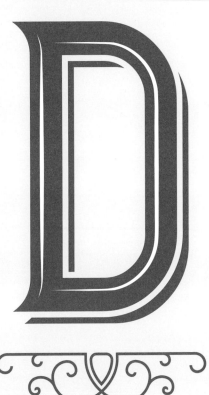

D

COCKNEY	ENGLISH
daffadowndilly	silly
Daily Mail	tale
daisy roots	boots – 'That's a smart pair of daisies.'
Danger Mouse	spouse
day's a-dawning	morning
dickory dock	clock
dicky bird	word (as in 'have a word')
dicky dirt	shirt – 'Where's me clean dicky?'
didn't ought	port
didgeridoo	screw (prison officer)
dig in the grave	shave
ding dong	song
ding dong bell	hell
dinky doo	twenty-two (bingo call)

Dame Edna Everage

beverage

Derry & Toms

bombs

Derry & Toms was a department store founded on Kensington High Street in London in 1860. It closed in 1973.

COCKNEY	ENGLISH
Doctor Crippen	dripping (as in 'bread and dripping')
dog and bone	phone
dog's knob	job
do me good(s)	Woods (Woodbines – cigarettes)
Duchess of Fife	wife ('She's me old Dutch.')
Duchess of York	chalk, cork, fork
duck and dive	hide
dustbin lids	kids

COCKNEY	ENGLISH
early hours	flowers
earwig	understand ('twig')
eighteen pence	sense
elephant's trunk	drunk

Euan Blair

Leicester Square

Former UK prime minister Tony Blair's
son, Euan, was arrested when he was
sixteen for being 'drunk and incapable'
in London's West End.

COCKNEY	ENGLISH
field of wheat	street
fife and drum	bum
fisherman's daughter	water – 'Gimme a drink of fisherman's.'
flowery dell	prison cell
Frasier Crane	pain
frog and toad	road – 'I'm going up the frog.'

fine and dandy

brandy

COCKNEY	ENGLISH
garden gate	magistrate
gay and frisky	whisky
gay and hearty	a party
George Michael	menstrual cycle
German bands	hands – 'Me Germans are freezing!'
ginger beer	engineer
give and take	cake
Glasgow Rangers	strangers
God forbids	kids – 'They're noisy godfors.'
goose's neck	cheque – 'I'll write you a goose's.'
Giorgio Armani	'sarnie' (sandwich)
grasshopper	copper
greengages	wages – 'I'll pay you back when I get me greens.'

Gordon & Gotch

watch

Established in Australia in 1853, Gordon &
Gotch was a company with a warehouse
in Plaistow, East London, from where they
distributed books, magazines and newspapers.
The company still exists today.

COCKNEY	ENGLISH
Hampstead Heath	teeth – 'Like me new 'ampsteads/'amps?'
Hampton Wick	prick (penis) – ''e gets on me Hampton!'
Harry Potter	'snotter' (nose)
Harry Randall	candle
Harvey Nichol	pickle (plight) – ''e's in a bit of a Harvey.'
Hearts of Oak	broke – 'Lend 'im a quid – 'e's 'arts.'
helter-skelter	air-raid shelter
hit and miss	piss, or kiss
holy friar	liar
Holy Ghost	*Racing Post*

Harvey Nichols

pickles

The luxury department store chain
Harvey Nichols was established in 1831.
Its flagship store is in Knightsbridge, London.

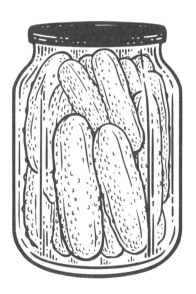

I

COCKNEY	ENGLISH
in and out	snout
Irish jig	wig
iron tank	bank
Isle of Wight	right
I suppose	nose

Ian Beale

real

Played by Adam Woodyatt, Ian Beale is a character in the BBC soap opera *EastEnders*.

J

COCKNEY	ENGLISH
Jack and Jill	hill, bill, till
jackdaw	jaw
Jack Dee	cup o' tea
Jackie Chan	can (of beer)
Jack Jones	alone – ''e's all on his Jack.'
Jack the Ripper	kipper
Jaffa Cake	mistake
jam jar	car
jam tart	fart
Jenson Button	mutton
Jerry O'Gorman	Mormon
Jimmy Riddle	piddle – 'I'm just going for a Jimmy.'
Jim Skinner	dinner
Joanna	pianner (piano)
Johnnie Horner	corner

Jack tar

bar

A 'Jack tar' is a seaman in Britain's Royal Navy or Merchant Navy. The term was especially prevalent during the time of the British Empire.

COCKNEY	ENGLISH
Kat Slater	catch yer later
Kate and Sidney	steak and kidney (as in a steak-and-kidney pie)
kidney punch	lunch
Khyber Pass	arse – ''e can stick that up his Khyber!')

Kate Carney

army – 'I'm joining the Kate.'

Born in 1869, Kate Carney was an English
music-hall singer and comedian in London.

L

COCKNEY	ENGLISH
la-di-dah	car
left jab	cab (taxi)
light and dark	park
Lilley & Skinner	dinner, also beginner
linen draper	paper (newspaper) – ''as the linen come yet?'
Lionel Messi	messy – 'Last night got a bit Lionel.'
lion's lair	chair
loaf of bread	head – 'Use yer loaf.'
loop the loop	soup – 'Gimme some more loopers.'
Lord Lovell	shovel
Lord Mayor	swear
Lousy Brown	Rose & Crown (a common pub name)
Lucy Locket	pocket

COCKNEY	ENGLISH
lump of ice	advice
lump of lead	head
lump of school	fool

Lillian Gish

fish

Gish was a pioneering American actress, born in 1893. Her seventy-five-year career in film began with silent movies in 1912 and ended only in 1987. She was known as the First Lady of American Cinema.

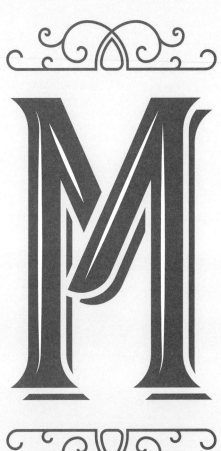

COCKNEY	ENGLISH
macaroni	a 'pony', i.e., £25
Marie Corelli	telly (television set)
merry-go-round	pound
Mickey Mouse	house
mince pies	eyes – 'She's got lovely minces.'
Molly Malone	phone
monkeys' tails	nails
Mother Hubbard	cupboard
Mother's ruin	gin
Mrs Chant	aunt

mozzle and brocha

'on the knocker', a door-to-door salesman

Mozzle is Yiddish for 'good luck'
and 'brocha' is a blessing.

N

COCKNEY	ENGLISH
nanny goat	boat, tote, coat
near and far	bar, car
needle and pin	gin
Neil Sedaka	parka
Newington Butts	guts – 'I 'it 'im in the Newingtons.'
Nigel Mansell	cancel
Noah's Ark	park, also 'nark' (an informer)
north and south	mouth

Nervo and Knox

pox, also 'gogglebox' (TV)

Jimmy Nervo and Teddy Knox
were an English comedy duo,
part of the original Crazy Gang.

O

COCKNEY	ENGLISH
ocean-going squid	quid
oily rag	fag (cigarette)
old pot and pan	'old man' (husband)
Oliver Twist	fist – ''e rammed 'is Oliver down 'is throat.'
Omar Sharif	grief
once a week	'beak' (magistrate)
on the floor	poor
orchestra stalls	balls (testicles) – 'It got 'im right in the orchestras.'
Otis Redding	wedding
Oxford scholar	dollar – 'Lend me an Oxford.'

Owen Nares

chairs

Nares was an English stage and
film actor born in 1888.

P.Q

COCKNEY	ENGLISH
peas in the pot	hot – 'It's a bit peasy in here.'
pen and ink	stink – 'It pens a bit.'
piccolo and flute	suit – 'That's a nice piccolo.'
pig and roast	toast
pig's ear	beer – 'I like me glass of pig's.'
pimple and blotch	Scotch (liquor)
pitch and toss	boss
plates of meat	feet – 'Mind me plates.'
pleasure and pain	rain

penny-come-quick

a trick

Recorded in Dodson and Saczek's *Dictionary of Cockney Rhyming Slang* in 1972, this originally meant a trick of any kind. It is now, according to *Green's Dictionary of Slang*, a UK underworld term for a 'confidence trick'.

COCKNEY	ENGLISH
rabbit and pork	talk – 'She can't 'alf rabbit!'
rank and riches	breeches
rats and mice	dice
rattle and clank	bank
Raquel Welch	belch
read and write	fight
Richard Burton	curtain – 'Draw the Richards.'
Richard the Third	bird (the feathered variety)
Rory O'More	door – 'Open the Rory!'
round the houses	trousers
rub-a-dub-dub	pub

Rosy Lea

tea – "ow about a cup of Rosy?"

Also spelled 'Rosie Lee', this rhyming slang
for tea was first recorded in *Soldier and Sailor
Words and Phrases*, published in 1925. Some
think it is a reference to American burlesque
entertainer Gypsy Rose Lee, but she was born
only in 1911, making that unlikely.

COCKNEY	ENGLISH
Salford Docks	rocks
salmon and trout	stout (beer)
satin and silk	milk
sausage and mash	cash, crash
Scapa Flow	go, scarper
Scooby-Doo	flu
Scotch mist	pissed (drunk)
Scotch pegs	legs – 'Cor, 'ave yer seen the 'airs on 'is Scotches?'
skin and blister	sister
sky rocket	pocket – 'Me skies are empty.'
sorry and sad	bad
stammer and stutter	butter
stand at ease	cheese

COCKNEY	ENGLISH
stand to attention	pension
supersonic	gin and tonic

Sexton Blake

cake – 'Pass the Sexton.'

Blake is a fictional detective who has
appeared in many British comic strips,
novels and dramas by hundreds of
different authors since 1893.

T

COCKNEY	ENGLISH
tea leaf	thief
teapot lid	quid (a pound), or kid
tick-tack	the track, racecourse
tiddlywink	drink – 'Come for a little tiddly.'
tit for tat	hat – 'I've got a new titfer.'
Toblerone	on my own
Tom and Dick	sick
Tom Thumb	rum
trouble and strife	wife – 'It's just the trouble and me at home.'
true till death	breath
tumble down the sink	drink
two and eight	state (of tension)

Tommy Tucker

supper

American blues artist Tommy Tucker's
hit song 'Hi-Heel Sneakers' rose to No. 23
in the UK singles chart in 1964.

U·V
W·Y

COCKNEY	ENGLISH
Uncle Bert	shirt – 'Why aven't you washed me uncle?'
Uncle Fred	bread
Uncle Ned	bed
weep and wail	a tail
weasel and stoat	coat – 'It's a bit parky. I'll put on my weasel.'
weeping willow	pillow
whistle and flute	suit – 'D'ye like me new whistle?'
yet to be	free
you and me	tea

Vera Lynn

gin

Dame Vera Lynn, who died in 2020, was known as the Forces' Sweetheart during the Second World War, during which she performed at outdoor concerts for troops in Egypt, India and Burma. Among her famous songs were 'We'll Meet Again', '(There'll Be Bluebirds Over) The White Cliffs of Dover' and 'A Nightingale Sang in Berkeley Square'.

ENGLISH

–

COCKNEY

ENGLISH	COCKNEY
advice	lump of ice
alone	Jack Jones
air-raid shelter	helter-skelter
arm	Chalk Farm
army	Kate Carney
arse	bottle and glass Khyber Pass
aunt	Mrs Chant

ENGLISH	COCKNEY
baby	basin of gravy
bad	sorry and sad
balls (testicles)	cobbler's awls orchestra stalls
bank	iron tank rattle and clank
bar (pub)	Jack Tar near and far
barrow	cock sparrow

ENGLISH	COCKNEY
beak (magistrate)	bubble and squeak once a week
beer	pig's ear
beginner	Lilley & Skinner
belch	Raquel Welch
believe	Adam and Eve
belly	Auntie Nellie
beverage	Dame Edna Everage
bike	clever mike
bill (account)	Beecham's pill Jack and Jill
bird (feathered)	Richard the Third
bitter (beer)	apple fritter
boat	nanny goat
boil	Conan Doyle
bombs	Derry & Toms

ENGLISH	COCKNEY
book	Captain Cook
boots	daisy roots
boss	pitch and toss
bottle	Aristotle
braces	airs and graces
brandy	fine and dandy
brandy and soda water	cockney breakfast
bread	Uncle Fred
breath	true till death
breeches	rank and riches
broke (financially)	Hearts of Oak coal and coke
bum	fife and drum
butter	stammer and stutter

ENGLISH	COCKNEY
cab (taxi)	left jab
cake	Sexton Blake give and take
can (of beer)	Jackie Chan
cancel	Nigel Mansell
candle	Harry Randall
cappuccino	Al Pacino
car	jam jar la-di-dah near and far
card	bladder of lard
cash	sausage and mash
cat	ball of fat
catch yer later	Kat Slater

ENGLISH	COCKNEY
cell (jail)	flowery dell
chair(s)	lion's lair Owen Nares
chalk	Duke of York
charlie (cocaine)	Bob Marley
cheese	stand at ease
cheque	goose's neck
clock	dickory dock
coach	cockroach
coat	weasel and stoat
code	à la mode
cold	taters in the mould
cook	babbling brook
copper	grasshopper
cork	Duke of York
corner	Johnnie Horner

ENGLISH	COCKNEY
crash	sausage and mash
crook	babbling brook
cupboard	Mother Hubbard
cup o' tea	Jack Dee
curtain	Richard Burton

ENGLISH	COCKNEY
dice	rats and mice
dinner	Jim Skinner Lilley & Skinner
dog	cherry hog
dole	Adrian Mole
dollar	Oxford scholar

ENGLISH	COCKNEY
door	Rory O'More
door-to-door salesman	mozzle and brocha
dozen	country cousin
drink	tiddlywink tumble down the sink
dripping	Dr Crippen
drunk	elephant's trunk

ENGLISH	COCKNEY
egg	borrow and beg
engineer	ginger beer
Epsom Races	airs and graces

ENGLISH	COCKNEY
face	Boat Race Chevy Chase
faces	airs and graces
fag (cigarette)	oily rag
fart	jam tart
feet	plates of meat
fight	read and write
fire	Anna Maria
fish	Lillian Gish
fist	Oliver Twist
fit	Brad Pitt
flowers	April showers, early hours
flu	Scooby-Doo

ENGLISH	COCKNEY
fool	lump of school
free	yet to be

ENGLISH	COCKNEY
geezer	Bacardi Breezer
get into trouble	cop a flower pot
gin	Mother's ruin
	needle and pin
	Vera Lynn
gin and soda water	cockney breakfast
gin and tonic	supersonic
go	Scapa Flow
gogglebox (TV)	Nervo and Knox

ENGLISH	COCKNEY
gravy	Army and Navy
grief	Omar Sharif
guts	Newington Butts
gutter	bread and butter

ENGLISH	COCKNEY
hair	Barnet Fair
hands	German bands
hat	tit for tat
head	crust of bread
	loaf of bread
	lump of lead
hell	ding dong bell

ENGLISH	COCKNEY
hide	duck and dive
hill	Jack and Jill
hot	peas in the pot
house	cat and mouse

ENGLISH	COCKNEY
jail	bucket and pail
jaw	jackdaw
job	dog's knob
judge	Barnaby Rudge

ENGLISH	COCKNEY
kids	God forbids dustbin lids teapot lids
kipper	Jack the Ripper
knees	biscuits and cheese

ENGLISH	COCKNEY
lark (joke)	Bushy Park
later	alligator
legs	Scotch pegs

ENGLISH	COCKNEY
Leicester Square	Euan Blair
liar	holy friar
liver	cheerful giver
lodger	Artful Dodger
London	Cockneyland
look	butcher's hook
lunch	kidney punch

ENGLISH	COCKNEY
magistrate	garden gate
married	cash and carried cut and carried
matches	cuts and scratches

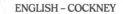

ENGLISH	COCKNEY
mate (friend)	china plate
messy	Lionel Messi
milk	Acker Bilk satin and silk
minute (time)	cock linnet
miss (a girl)	cuddle and kiss
mistake	Jaffa Cake
moans	Catherine Zeta-Jones
money	bees and honey
Mormon	Jerry O'Gorman
morning	day's a-dawning
mouth	north and south
muttton	Jenson Button

ENGLISH	COCKNEY
nails	monkey's tails
nark	Noah's Ark
neck	bushel and peck
noise	box of toys
nose	I suppose

ENGLISH	COCKNEY
old man (husband)	old pot and pan
on my own	Toblerone
on the Labour	beggar my neighbour

ENGLISH	COCKNEY
pain	Frasier Crane
pants	Adam and the Ants
paper (newspaper)	linen draper
park	Noah's Ark
parka	Neil Sedaka
party	gay and hearty
penny	Abergavenny
pension	stand to attention
phone	dog and bone Molly Malone
piano	Joanna
pickle (plight)	Harvey Nichol
pickles	Harvey Nichols

ENGLISH	COCKNEY
piddle	Jimmy Riddle
pillow	weeping willow
piss	hit and miss
pissed	Scotch mist
pocket	Lucy Locket sky rocket
police officer	bottle and stopper, 'copper'
'pony' (£25)	macaroni
port	didn't ought
pound	merry-go-round
pox	Nervo and Knox
prick	Hampton Wick
pub	rub-a-dub-dub
pyjamas	Barack Obama

ENGLISH	COCKNEY
quid	ocean-going squid teapot lid

ENGLISH	COCKNEY
racecourse (track)	tick-tack
Racing Post	Holy Ghost
rain	Andy Cain pleasure and pain
real	Ian Beale
rent	Burton-on-Trent

ENGLISH	COCKNEY
right	Isle of Wight
road	frog and toad
Rose & Crown (pub)	Lousy Brown
row	bull and cow
rubber (condom)	advice from Mother
rum	Tom Thumb

ENGLISH	COCKNEY
saloon bar	balloon car
sarnie (sandwich)	Giorgio Armani
saw (tool)	bear's paw
say-so	cocoa

ENGLISH	COCKNEY
Scotch (liquor)	pimple and blotch
scouts	Brussels' sprouts
screw (prison officer)	didgeridoo
sense	eighteen pence
shave	dig in the grave
ship	'apenny dip
shirt	Dicky Dirt Uncle Bert
shovel	Lord Lovell
sick	Tom and Dick
silly	daffadowndilly
sister	skin and blister
six (bingo call)	chop sticks
sixty-six (bingo call)	clickety-click
skint (broke)	boracic lint
sleep	Bo-Peep

ENGLISH	COCKNEY
sneeze	bread and cheese
snotter (nose)	Harry Potter
snout	in and out
soap	Cape of Good Hope
socks	almond rocks
son	Bath bun currant bun
song	ding dong
soup	loop the loop
sparrow(s)	bow and arrow(s)
spouse	Danger Mouse
stairs	apples and pears
state (tension)	two and eight
steak and kidney	Kate and Sidney
still (photograph)	Beecham's pill
stink	pen and ink

ENGLISH	COCKNEY
stools	April Fool's
stout (beer)	salmon and trout
strangers	Glasgow Rangers
street	field of wheat
stunner	air gunner
suit	piccolo and flute whistle and flute
suitcase	crowded place
sun	Bath bun currant bun
supper	Tommy Tucker
swear	Lord Mayor

ENGLISH	COCKNEY
table	Cain and Abel
talk	rabbit and pork
tale	*Daily Mail*
tea	Rosy Lea
tears	Britney Spears
teeth	Hampstead Heath
telly	custard and jelly Marie Corelli
thief	tea leaf
ticket	bat and wicket
till (cash)	Jack and Jill
time	bird lime
'titty'	Bristol City

ENGLISH	COCKNEY
toast	pig and roast
tools	April Fool's
tote	canal boat nanny goat
treadmill	can't keep still
trick	penny-come-quick
twenty-two (bingo)	dinky doo

ENGLISH	COCKNEY
umbrella	Auntie Ella
understand ('twig')	earwig

ENGLISH	COCKNEY
wages	greengages
walk	ball of chalk
wash	Bob Squash
watch	Gordon & Gotch
water	fisherman's daughter
wedding	Otis Redding
whisky	gay and frisky
wife	bag for life carving knife Duchess of Fife trouble and strife
wig	Irish jig
window	burnt cinder

ENGLISH	COCKNEY
Woods/Woodbines (cigarettes)	**do me goods**
word	**dicky bird**